P9-CPV-890

Ripley's Believe It or Not!

SPECIAL EDITION 2008

Scholastic Inc.
New York   Toronto   London   Auckland   Sydney
Mexico City   New Delhi   Hong Kong   Buenos Aires

Copyright © 2007 by Ripley Entertainment Inc.
All rights reserved. Ripley's, Ripley's Believe It or Not!, Believe It or Not!, and Believe It! are registered trademarks of Ripley Entertainment Inc. Published by Scholastic Inc. SCHOLASTIC and associated logos are trademarks and/or registered trademarks of Scholastic Inc.

No part of this publication may be reproduced in whole or in part, or stored in a retrieval system, or transmitted in any form or by any means, electronic, mechanical, photocopying, recording, or otherwise, without written permission of the publisher. For information regarding permission, write to Scholastic Inc., Attention: Permissions Department, 557 Broadway, New York, NY 10012.

Library of Congress Cataloging-in-Publication data is available

ISBN-13: 978-0-439-92059-9
ISBN-10: 0-439-92059-0

Developed and produced by Miles Kelly Publishing Ltd
in association with Ripley Publishing

Publishing Director: Anne Marshall
Art Director: Jo Brewer
Project Editor: Rosie Alexander
Managing Editor: Becky Miles
Editorial Assistant: Gemma Simmons
Designer: Jim Marks

12 11 10 9 8 7 6 5 4 3 2 1   7 8 9 10 11/0

Printed in China

First printing, September 2007

CONTENTS

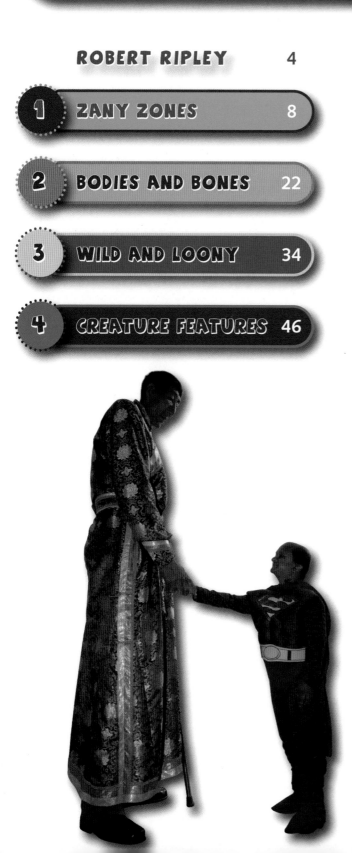

ROBERT RIPLEY

ROBERT RIPLEY was working for the *New York Globe* newspaper in 1918 as a sports columnist when he had the idea of drawing cartoons that concentrated on the weird and bizarre, and people's extraordinary achievements. The cartoon was given the title "Believe It or Not!" to reflect the incredible but true stories that Ripley unearthed. It proved an instant success, and he went on to travel all over the world, collecting weird artifacts and bizarre facts and feats.

FAR AND WILD

Ripley loved to travel, and by 1940 he had visited no fewer than 201 countries. One of his amazing journeys included 15,000 miles by air, 8,000 miles by ship, and over 1,000 miles by camel, horse, and donkey—all to seek out stories for the 80 million people who read his Believe It or Not! cartoons.

ROBERT RIPLEY encouraged readers to send stories and photographs, from which he drew his cartoons. He sometimes received over 170,000 letters a week! One was from a boy revealing how his pet beagle regularly ate shards of glass. Ripley published the boy's drawing. The boy was a young Charles Schulz, and the beagle became the inspiration for Snoopy.

Ripley's — Believe It or Not!

WACKY WORLD

Although Robert Ripley died in 1949, his eager researchers continue to scour the globe for stories about amazing animals, fantastic festivals, freaky feats, haunted horrors, and crazy creations. Believe It or Not, there are hundreds of mind-boggling facts in this book alone!

Metal Magic, U.S.A., page 13

What a Mug! Key West, Florida, page 36

Sitting Pretty, China, page 81

Heads Start, China, page 58

Atlantic City, New Jersey

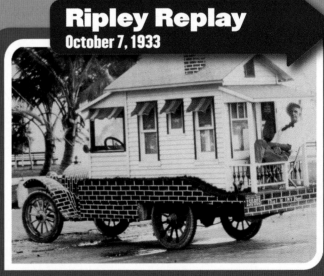

HOUSE OF FUN

Ripley's first museum (or Odditorium) was built in Chicago in 1933, and there are now 29 throughout the world. The second oldest (seen above) is in Niagara Falls, Ontario, and was opened in 1963. It houses such weird exhibits as a Jivaro Indian shrunken torso and a lamb with a horn!

"ROLLING HOME"
CHARLES MILLER LIVED AND TRAVELED IN HIS OWN HOME FOR 2 YEARS, 8 MONTHS AND 8 DAYS
The House is 3 ft, 9 in. Wide and 6 ft. Long.

TOON TALK

Ripley's has a vast computer database of facts and a massive photographic archive. These black-and-white photographs (the basis for Ripley's cartoons) appear in the "Ripley Replay" features in this book. The date accompanying the photograph is the date the cartoon was first published.

Ripley Replay
October 7, 1933

Charles Miller lived in his mobile home, 6 feet by 3 feet 9 inches, for nearly three years.

1

ZANY ZONES

AT LARGE

TROLL BRIDGE

Lurking beneath the Aurora Bridge in Seattle, Washington, is a huge sculpture of a scary, long-haired troll. Although you can see only his head and shoulders, the sculpture, which was created by four local artists in 1990, is 18 feet tall. He has a shiny metal eye and is crushing a full-size Volkswagen Beetle in his left hand. He may look fearsome but Seattle residents are so fond of him that they stage a "Trollaween" party every October 31.

BIG FOOT

There's a wooden roller skate near Warrenton, Virginia, more than 9 feet tall! So if you ever visit, you'll probably need to stand on someone's shoulders just to see over the top!

POT LUCK

If you need a big cup of coffee, the place to go is Stanton, Iowa. To celebrate the fact that it was the home of Mrs. Olson, of Folgers Coffee TV commercials, in 1971 the town erected a giant Swedish-style coffee pot that was painted with hearts and flowers. Perched on top of a 90-foot tower, the pot is 35 feet high and holds 40,000 gallons. There is even a similar-sized coffee cup nearby.

DYETHINKESAURUS?

Don't even think about driving through the California desert if you are scared of dinosaurs. Towering over the side of Highway 10 at Cabazon, near Palm Springs, is a scene straight out of Jurassic Park—two amazing 65-foot-tall prehistoric beasts! Named Dinny and Mr. Rex, they were constructed by the late Claude K. Bell as a roadside attraction and have been featured in Coca-Cola commercials, rock videos, and feature films.

Ripley Replay
February 13, 1932

The California Piano Supply Co. decided to go for music in a big way with this grand piano!

11

WACKY WAY

WHERE AM I?

Visitors to Watson Lake, Yukon, Canada, could be forgiven for feeling confused about where they are. That's because it is home to Sign Post Forest, a collection of more than 10,000 town signs from all over the world. The first sign was put up in 1942 by a homesick U.S. G.I., Carl K. Lindley of Danville, Illinois, who was there while working on the Alaska Highway. Others soon followed his lead and to this day the tradition continues.

WHAT A GAS!

Built in the 1950s, a cowboy-themed gas station near Seattle, Washington, featured a building topped by a cowboy hat with a 44-foot-wide brim and a pair of giant boots that served as the men's and ladies' toilets.

GOPHER IT?

About ten years ago so many ground squirrels, or gophers, were wreaking havoc around the Canadian farming hamlet of Torrington, Alberta, that someone decided to put the dead ones to good use. To attract tourists, they set up the Gopher Hole Museum, which features 77 stuffed gophers wearing handmade costumes in nearly 50 different settings that give a humorous view of life in a small Alberta town.

METAL MAGIC

If you take a drive down the 32-mile stretch of road between Regent and Gladstone, North Dakota, you may feel a little smaller than usual. That's because the road, known as the Enchanted Highway, is lined with huge metal sculptures. Created by Gary Greff, they include a 60-foot grasshopper, a tin family, and a family of pheasants with a 70-foot-long rooster, a 60-foot hen, and 15-foot-high chicks!

Ripley Replay
October 10, 1936

Amazingly, this house is made of salt and doesn't dissolve in the rain!

MONUMENTAL

PAPER HOUSE

You're never short of something to read at one house in Rockport, Massachusetts. That's because it's constructed entirely from recycled newspapers. Each wall is made of 215 reinforced layers of the stuff. Not surprisingly, there isn't a fireplace.

MIRROR, MIRROR

In Chicago, Illinois, you can almost have your head in the clouds while standing on the ground! It's all thanks to Cloud Gate, a 110-ton bean-shaped sculpture by British artist Anish Kapoor. Inspired by liquid mercury and built from highly polished stainless steel plates, it reflects the famous Chicago skyline and the clouds above like a huge curved mirror. When you walk under its 12-foot arch, it's a mind-bending experience: your reflection is pulled and stretched over the smooth surface as in a house of mirrors.

BLOW-UP CHURCH

Couples can now get married wherever they want in the world, thanks to an inflatable church developed in England. The church is 39 feet high and takes two hours to inflate. It can seat 60 people, has plastic "stained glass" windows and airbrush artwork to make it look like the real thing. Inside, there is an inflatable organ, altar, pulpit, pews, candles, and a gold cross. Even the doors are flanked by air-filled angels. But the minister has to be genuine.

HOLY HIPPOS!

You might possibly expect to find hippopotamus teeth in a museum or on an African safari, but not in the walls of an Italian monastery. Yet the Certosa di Pavia, near Milan, has a fifteenth-century sacristy—the area of a cathedral that houses the sacred vessels for Holy Communion—that was built entirely out of hippo teeth! Hippos must have pretty strong teeth—it's been standing for 600 years.

Ripley Replay
December 18, 1936

This car is covered in 37,700 stamps from 60 different countries.

15

What in the World

SECRET SPACE

Deep below the Mulu Mountains in Malaysia is a cave called the Sarawak Chamber. It is so huge that it could hold the White House, the Capitol Building, and Washington D.C.'s National Mall inside!

River Riddle

There is a river in India that flows in both directions at the same time! During the rainy season, the surface of the Baleswar River flows southward while its lower currents run in a northerly direction.

FOSSIL FOREST

The Petrified Forest in Arizona features a landscape of fossilized trees of stone sparkling like gems in all the colors of the rainbow. It was formed 225 million years ago when tall conifers fell and were coated with mud, sand, volcanic ash, and silica-rich water.

HAIL HAVOC

In July 2002, hailstones the size of hens' eggs fell in Henan province, China. The hailstones were falling so hard that they smashed car windows, destroyed buildings, and killed 25 people. Many others were rushed to hospitals with serious head injuries.

FOR THE BIRDS

On Peru's Guano Islands, fish-eating birds had produced mountains of dung that were hundreds of feet high by the time people began harvesting it for fertilizer in the nineteenth century.

Great Balls of Fire

When a bolt of lightning hits the ground, it sometimes creates an amazing, but potentially deadly, fireball. These glowing balls can float up to six feet above the ground for a few minutes before going out with a hiss, or a loud bang.

STONE GHOSTS

Visitors to the White Desert in Bahariya, Egypt, are often amazed by the beautiful sculptures. But these domes and castles aren't manmade! They are actually composed of chalk that has been exposed to years of weathering. It is this natural erosion that has created the limestone shapes.

VALUABLE VOLCANO

A volcano that is situated 39,000 feet below the surface of the Bismarck Sea, off Papua New Guinea, emits tiny amounts of molten silver and gold when it erupts.

THE GRUMBLING MOUNTAIN

Can you believe it? There is actually a mountain that roars. The Sand Mountain of Fallon, Nevada, is composed of sharp, fine, white sand. When the particles of sand are moved by the wind, they rub together and make a rumbling sound. The noise can be heard from miles away.

FRIENDLY GIANTS

PETAL POWER

Planted in a pool behind El Museo Nacional de Bellas Artes in Buenos Aires, Argentina, is one of the world's strangest flowers. In fact, it's not really a flower at all, but an 18-ton steel magnolia—a beautiful reflective sculpture made from aluminum and steel. "Floralis generica" (the generic flower) was designed by Eduardo Catalano, an Argentinian architect who trained in the U.S., and was presented to the city in 2002. Each petal is over 60 feet high and reflects the rippling water beneath. And just like many real plants, it closes at night. A hydraulic device opens the petals at dawn and closes them at sunset.

BIG HEAD!

Australian sculptor Ron Mueck specializes in extravagantly sized works that explore the full life cycle of humans. They can be strange to look at, especially since he likes to play around with the scale of his models. At his 2006 exhibition in Edinburgh, Scotland, he unveiled a man with a huge head on a normal-sized body. He also made a sculpture of a newborn baby girl that was an alarming 16 feet long, while in another room, he displayed a couple of adults that were no bigger than dolls. Each sculpture requires a lot of preparation. He begins with drawings and clay models before making a fiberglass cast. Attention to detail is really important—for example, body hair is painstakingly attached to his human models, strand by strand.

Living Doll

Over a period of four days in May 2006, the streets of London, England, were brought to a standstill by a 16-foot-tall girl and a 42-ton mechanical elephant. The whole event was planned in great secrecy. The first hint of the extraordinary things to come didn't occur until the morning of May 4, when a wooden rocket was found "crashed" in a Westminster street. One driver was so amazed that he nearly drove into a lamppost! As news spread that the strange craft would be opened the next afternoon, hundreds gathered to see the giant girl puppet emerge and walk around the city, operated every step of the way by skilled puppeteers. She rode a huge scooter and spent the night sleeping in a giant deckchair in a park. She even gave children rides in her hand. Meanwhile the 40-foot elephant, made from hundreds of moving parts and built mainly of wood, also began thundering along the streets, spraying passersby with water as it did so. On the last day, the girl climbed back into her spaceship, which closed and then reopened to reveal that she had disappeared. People were in tears as she waved good-bye and were stunned when she vanished.

SUPERSIZE ME!

JUMBO COOKIE

Imagine biting into a cookie that weighs more than four huge elephants! Well, in 2003, a massive 36,000-pound chocolate chip cookie was cooked and unveiled by the Immaculate Baking Company at Flat Rock, North Carolina. The giant cookie was 100 feet in diameter, which is about the size of a basketball court or the length of a Boeing 737. It took around six hours to bake in a specially modified oven.

SLICE FOR EVERYONE

A company in Edmonton, Alberta, Canada, made a Christmas log cake that weighed 5,500 pounds and was 72 feet long. It was so big, there was enough to feed 3,500 guests!

PANAMANIAN PAN

No ordinary stove could have handled the saucepan that was created in Panama City in 2003. At more than 6 feet tall, the giant pan had to be carefully positioned on a series of high bricks, which towered over all the cooks. The saucepan wasn't exactly cooking dinner for one—it held over 2,000 tons of soup! And that required a lot of soup bowls.

BIG KISS

Kisses don't come any bigger than the one prepared by the French Culinary Institute and pastryscoop.com of New York in 2003. They sculpted a Hershey's Kisses dark chocolate that was 6 ½ feet tall and 6 feet wide. The giant Kiss, weighing in at around 6,340 pounds, was equivalent to approximately 639,636 of their regular-size Kisses. That's one heck of a kiss!

RICH DARK

Ripley Replay
September 21, 1954

WORLD'S LARGEST SHORTCAKE 1954 LEBANON ORE. 1954

12,000 people helped themselves to a piece of this 5,358-pound shortcake in Oregon.

C
COAMCO
266-4202

2

BODIES AND BONES

HYST-TORICAL!

CRANI-ODD-OMY?

For a century, historians have been trying to discover what happened to the skull of the famous American Indian leader Geronimo, who died in 1909. Recently discovered letters have suggested that Geronimo's skull may have been removed from its tomb by members of Yale University's top secret Skull and Bones Society. One of the chief culprits is believed to have been President George W. Bush's grandfather! The story could be true, but a lot of people still have their doubts.

FREAKY FORENSICS

We all know that Beethoven was deaf, but did you also know that he died of lead poisoning? That's what scientists at an Illinois laboratory discovered in 2000 by taking X-rays of his hair and skull. They showed that the composer, who died in 1827, suffered long-term lead poisoning, probably caused by diet or medication. The bone fragment used in the study belongs to a Californian businessman who inherited it from an Austrian doctor.

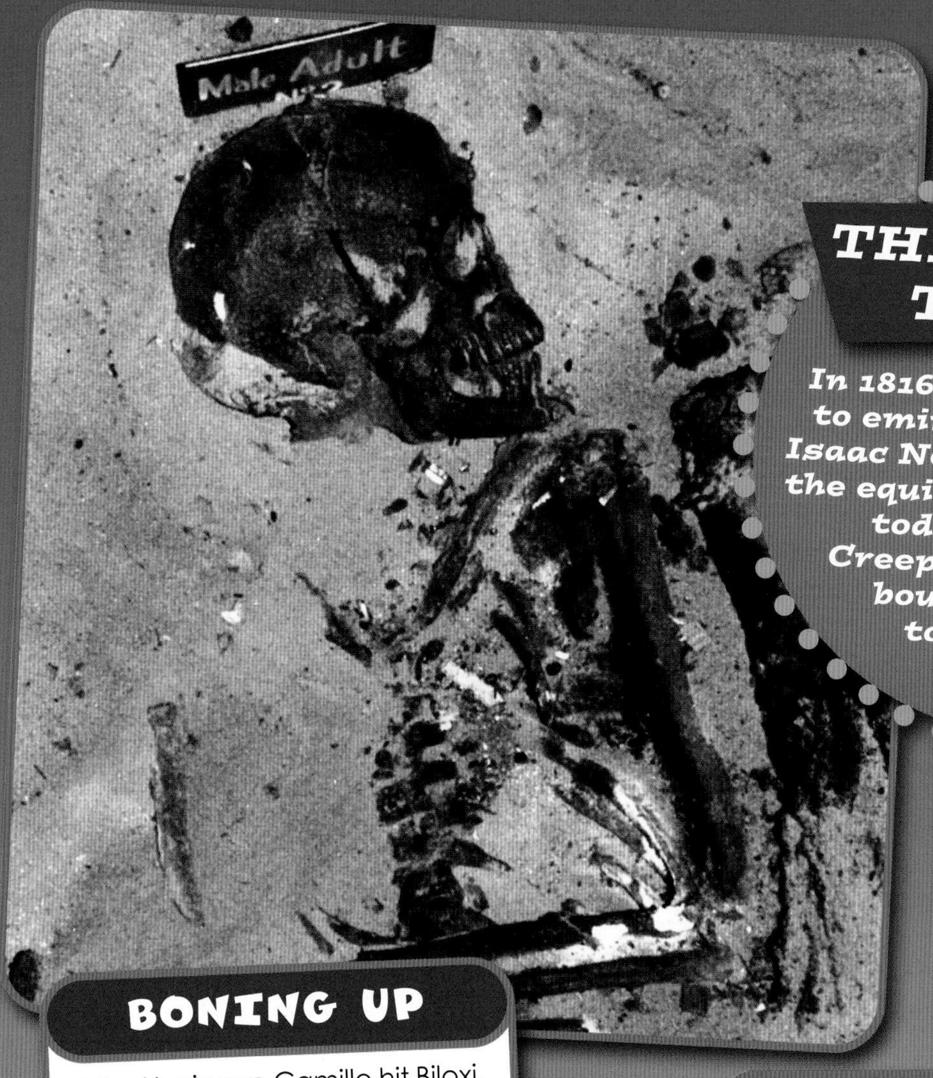

Male Adult Nº3

In 1816, a tooth belonging to eminent scientist Sir Isaac Newton was sold, for the equivalent of $35,700 in today's currency. Creepily, the man who bought it had the tooth set in a ring!

BONING UP

After Hurricane Camille hit Biloxi, Mississippi, in 1969, 13 ancient skeletons were found beneath the floorboards of artist Joe Moran's studio. Adjacent pots and other artifacts suggested that they might date back to 2200 BCE. What did he do with them? Instead of donating them to a museum, he decided to leave them in place and built a Plexiglas window in the floor so that visitors could view his remarkable find.

Ripley Replay
Exact date unknown

Trepanning, evidence of a form of brain surgery, has been found in 40,000-year-old skulls.

25

OLD BOYS

DEAD FAMOUS

In 2005, nearly 200 years after his death, scientists discovered what might have caused King George III of the United Kingdom to go mad. Toward the end of his reign, George III had regular bouts of mental illness and, to control his wild behavior, spent time in a straitjacket chained to a chair. When three strands of his hair were found in a British museum, they were chemically analyzed and found to contain abnormally high levels of arsenic—17 times more than the amount needed just to poison him. It's thought that the actual medicine used to treat his depression might have contained the arsenic. No wonder, then, that poor old George's behavior was erratic.

MOST FOUL

With the Soviet army closing in on his Berlin bunker on April 30, 1945, German dictator Adolf Hitler committed suicide. In accordance with his last orders, his body was burned. When the Russians arrived, all they found were charred pieces of Hitler's skull and his teeth. Amazingly, at the Moscow archives where Hitler's remains were kept, the pieces of his skull were stored on two pieces of Kleenex in a floppy disk container! Nearly 60 years later, Hitler's remains were put on display in Moscow. Subsequently, the teeth were identified as authentic by comparing them to X-rays of Hitler's skull taken in 1944, which revealed that he suffered from bad tooth decay. This in turn confirmed a little known fact about Hitler: that he suffered from bad breath. That's what people close to him often used to complain—but not to his face!

Beau Bog Men

In a peat bog in Ireland, in 2003, two well-preserved mummies were found. Both the male bodies had been brutally murdered more than 2,000 years ago. The pair were named after the places in which they were found: Clonycavan and Croghan Hill, just 25 miles apart. Tests showed that they lived between the fourth and second centuries BCE. Clonycavan man (as seen above in the reconstructed head) was only 5 feet 2 inches tall and, possibly to make himself look a little taller, he wore an early form of hair gel. It was made of vegetable plant oil mixed with resin from pine trees found in Spain and southwest France. Although missing his head and lower limbs, Old Croghan man was believed to be 6 feet 6 inches tall. He had very well-manicured nails and his hands were still in remarkably good condition. Scientists said his fingerprints were as clear as any living person's. Amazingly, scientists were also able to determine what Old Croghan man had eaten for his final supper: buttermilk and cereal!

STILL LIVES

STONE TRIBUTE

Most cemetery headstones are simple but occasionally you find something really unusual. Like in Israel where a 17-year-old boy is remembered by a tombstone in the shape of a large cell phone. At a cemetery in Barre, Vermont, headstones have been carved in the shape of an empty chair, even a soccer ball. The grave of local driver Joey Laquerre Jr., who died in 1991, is guarded by a half-size stone replica of his race car, number 61.

BIZARRE COFFINS

Who wants to spend the afterlife in the belly of a shark? They do in Ghana, but you don't have to worry—the shark is not real, but made of wood. Funerals in Ghana are colorful affairs and coffins are often relevant to the life of the dead person. That's why a company designs special wooden coffins in the shape of a lobster (for a fisherman), a running shoe (for an athlete), and the shark—maybe for someone who doesn't want many mourners!

HEAVY SEAS

People looking for a unique place to be buried can have their ashes put in artificial concrete reefs off the coast of Florida or South Carolina. Not only is the ocean a nice place to rest, but the reefs are good for the environment too.

BIG BANG

Popular American writer Hunter S. Thompson was determined to go out with a bang. Before his death in February 2005, he asked to be cremated and for his ashes to be fired from a cannon. In a spectacular fireworks display, his remains were shot into the sky from a 153-foot tower built behind his home in Woody Creek, Colorado. About 250 guests observed the launch of Thompson's ashes.

Ripley Replay
September 11, 1934

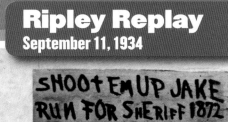

Lying low in Boot Hill Cemetery.

Mummies and Daddies

MUMMY MYSTERY

The 1,500-year-old mummy of a woman found in Peru had tattoos of spiders, snakes, and religious and magical figures. Beside her in her tomb were jewels, and necklaces and earrings in gold, copper, and silver.

GHOST SHIP

In 2006, a ghost ship washed ashore in Barbados. The phantom crew was made up of the corpses of 11 men. They had been partially petrified (turned to stone) by the salt water, sun, and sea breezes of the Atlantic Ocean.

REWRITING HISTORY

Italian archaeologists digging in the Roman Forum recently found a well-preserved skeleton of a woman who lived 3,000 years ago. The amazing thing about that is it dates back to at least 300 years before the traditional founding of Rome, 753 BC.

FROZEN STIFF

Two climbers in the Alps discovered a glacier-mummy — a freeze-dried man. "Otzi," as he was called, had been preserved in ice for around 5,000 years at an altitude of about 10,000 feet.

DOUBLE McMUMMY!

In 2001, two Egyptian mummies were discovered under a McDonald's restaurant! They are thought to have been buried in Tamworth, England, in the 1930s, by a collector.

MUMMY FOR SALE

You can buy some weird things on the Internet auction site eBay, but surely nothing stranger than a mummified human! Yet that was what a Michigan woman tried to sell in 2006. One person bid $500 before eBay removed the posting because it violated their policy against selling human remains.

REMAINS OF THE DAY

Archaeologists digging at a burial site near Cairo, Egypt, in 2003 found mummies that are believed to be over 5,000 years old! One mummy could be the oldest male mummy ever found.

SPOOKY

English vacationers looking for unusual souvenirs have been buying real human bones at a former seaside tea shop in Newquay, Cornwall. Items such as skulls, leg bones, vertebrae, and ribs are on sale.

SKELETON STAFF

At a school in Romania, teachers use the skeleton of an old headmaster to help with anatomy lessons! Former principal Grigore Alexandru Popescu wrote in his will that he wanted to donate his body to education. It is believed he also put a curse on anyone who tried to move the skeleton from the school.

BONE IDOLS

Each November, Mexicans celebrate the Day of the Dead, when, according to folklore, the deceased come back to life. Families decorate skeletons and hold graveside picnics where they eat chocolate coffins!

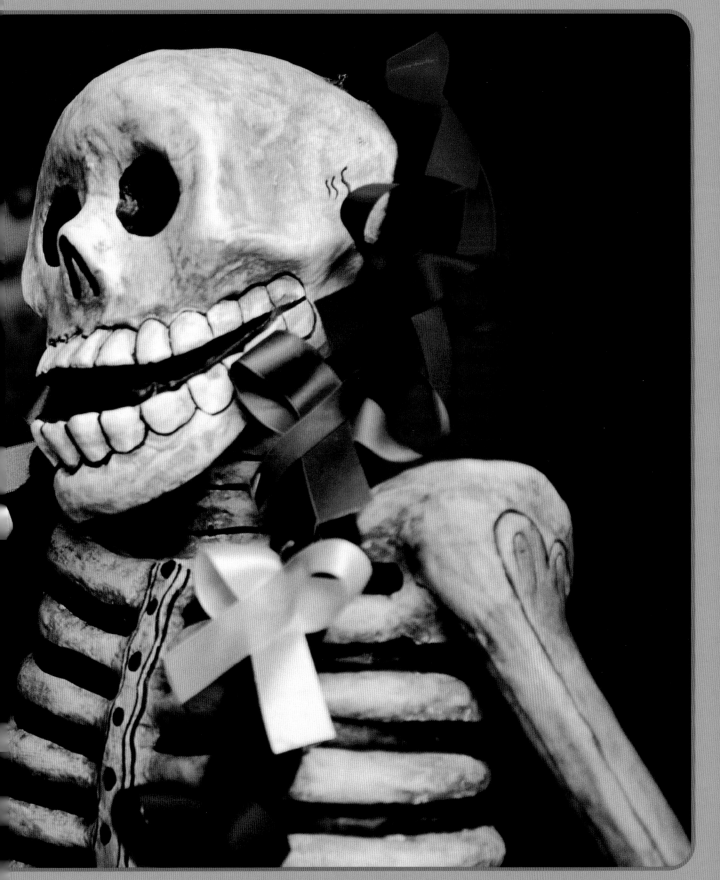

3

WILD AND LOONY

GOOFY!

WHAT A MUG!

Each year in Key West, Florida, there is a beauty pageant with a difference. Dogs and cats, dressed in wigs and jackets, compete by being dressed up to look like humans. There is also a lookalike pet and owner contest. First prize goes to the pet and its owner that look as if they could have been separated at birth. No prizes for guessing that Todd Heins won for painting his face and hair to resemble his pet Mexican green iguana, Miss Trouble!

HOT STUFF

In Beaver, Oklahoma, competitors hurl sun-dried cow chips distances of nearly 500 feet. It's no use complaining if the throw's not long enough—what's dung is dung!

OODLES OF NOODLES!

Li Enhai is just nutty about noodles. In November 2005, he took part in a noodle-pulling contest in China, during which he made more than two million noodles, all the same length. Lined end-to-end, they equaled a total of 1,648 miles—that's about the length of 63 marathon races, six times the length of the Grand Canyon, or about the same distance as from Los Angeles to New Orleans. That's a staggering whole heap of noodles!

FEE, FIE, FOE, FUM

Only a giant who hadn't eaten for a month could manage to devour India's biggest poori. Prepared in a huge frying pan as part of a competition, the winning poori (a deep-fried flat brown bread) measured 4.3 feet in diameter! The metal spatula used to stop the poori from sticking to the pan was big enough to row a boat with!

Ripley Replay
April 26. 1941

This frying pan, 9 feet 6 inches wide, was used to fry thousands of clams for 5,500 people!

UNDERACHIEVERS!

WATER MUSIC

When Handel composed his "Water Music," he had no idea that it might serve as the inspiration for a wacky festival that takes place in the Florida Keys each year. At the Lower Keys Underwater Music Festival, staged six miles off the coast, as many as 600 divers and snorkelers play musical instruments such as the staghorn and trombonefish, the manta-lin, and the fiddle crab! Other sights include an underwater symphony (conducted by a diver using a snorkel as a baton), a trio of divas of the deep, and a long-haired mermaid with a harp.

DEEP SHELL-TER

In the 1830s, so one story goes, two children were playing in their garden in Margate, England, when the ground gave way and they found themselves in an underground grotto. Its walls were covered with millions of shells to form a beautiful 2,000-square-foot mosaic. Today, the Shell Grotto is open to the public, but its origins still remain a mystery. Some think it could have been constructed as recently as the nineteenth century, but others believe it dates back over 2,000 years to pre-Roman times.

Under-Cutters

Thousands of people across the United States carve pumpkins for Halloween. Most do it in the kitchen, in the yard, or, at the very least, on dry land. But every October, a group of diving enthusiasts disappear some 25 feet beneath the surface of the ocean in the Florida Keys National Marine Sanctuary to carve pumpkins underwater. The original idea for the Underwater Pumpkin Carving Contest was thought up by Amy Slate's Amoray Dive Resort. Contestants are given a hollowed-out pumpkin to take below the surface. Using their dive knives as carving tools, they then have to create the most impressive jack-o'-lantern while squatting on the ocean bed in full diving gear. They are judged on design originality, steadiness of carving hand, and scuba skills. They get to show off their efforts in a setting surrounded by yellowtail snapper, queen angelfish, and beautiful coral, with prizes going to the sculptors of the best three pumpkins.

Wicked!

CABLE CAPER

A burglar looting the 22nd floor of a skyscraper in China tied a cable around his waist and jumped out the window to escape. He spent the next two hours dangling on the too-short cable until he could be rescued!

NAPPING ON THE JOB

A thief was caught when he fell asleep in an empty coffin after burglarizing a funeral home in Canton, New York!

A FAIR COP

A man from Barrie, Canada, who pretended to be a traffic policeman was sent to jail after he made the mistake of pulling over a real detective for speeding.

POINTING THE FINGER

A vandal who knocked over 53 headstones in a New York State cemetery left behind a small but important clue—his finger. The severed digit end was found between two toppled gravestones. A man missing a finger was quickly found and arrested.

A man in Virginia committed two bank robberies in a day. He got away the first time but was arrested after the second because he made his getaway in a commercial van that had his name marked clearly on the side.

BUNGLING BANDIT

A bungling bank robber in Swansea, Massachusetts, fainted when the teller he held up said she had no money. He came to and tried to escape, but he had locked his keys inside the getaway car!

LOST TEETH

An Argentinian robber was caught after he lost his false teeth during a raid on a house. The dentures were handed over to police who were able to match them to the toothless suspect.

WHAT A GIVEAWAY!

After stealing cash from a Colorado Springs store, a robber demanded a bottle of whiskey from the shelf. The clerk refused to serve him because he didn't think he was 21. To prove he was, the robber showed the clerk his driver's license—which had his full name and address.

FATAL ATTRACTION

A man wanted by the police was arrested when his parole officer spotted him kissing his girlfriend in a live crowd shot displayed on the scoreboard at a Cincinnati Reds baseball game. Of the 30,000 people in the ballpark, the camera operator just happened to hone in on him.

This is Elmar Weisser with his prize-winning windmill beard at the 2006 International Beard Championships in Germany. His biggest problem must be getting through doors.

PARTY ON!

SKIN DEEP

Every August in the Spanish town of Buñol, thousands of people wade through the streets waist-deep in mushy tomatoes. It's all part of La Tomatina, an annual festival dating back over sixty years in which competitors pelt each other with 150,000 pounds of over-ripe tomatoes for an hour and a half. It looks great fun but, for many, the best bit is being hosed down at the end.

HOT SOCKS

Each spring in Annapolis, Maryland, boaters burn their smelly old socks in a special ceremony to celebrate the start of warm weather. Visitors are advised to stand upwind of the fire.

THAT'S WILD!

At the Wild Foods Festival in Hokitika, New Zealand, you can sample such delicacies as possum pâté, ostrich pie, deep-fried fish eyes, and earthworm casserole! A particular favorite is the huhu grub, a delicacy that lives in rotting wood and eventually grows into a beetle. The grubs can be barbecued, dipped in chocolate, or served plain. The festival organizers say the grubs taste like peanut butter. It's probably best to take their word for it.

SAY CHEESE!

Believe it or not, these guys are chasing cheese! They are taking part in the annual cheese-rolling contest at Cooper's Hill, Gloucestershire, England. The starter releases a large Double Gloucester cheese down the steep hill and the competitors race after it. The winner's prize is the cheese itself. It may sound like harmless fun, but chasing cheese can be dangerous. Due to the gradient and the slippery grass, injuries are common, and every year people end up with broken bones.

Ripley Replay
November 25, 1933

Though blind, New Yorker Augustine Massa won 27 games of checkers simultaneously.

4

CREATURE FEATURES

THAT'S NOT NORMAL!

THE DAREDEVIL DOG

Like most dogs, Brutus the Californian dachshund enjoys the high life. In fact the life he enjoys is at a height of 15,000 feet with his human skydiving partner, Ron Sirull. Wearing specially made goggles, Brutus has made over 100 jumps, each time tucked into a pooch pouch fastened to Ron's chest. Ron says the only part Brutus doesn't enjoy is the sound of the plane taking off. "So I cup my hands around his ears," he says.

KISS KISS, HISS HISS!

Some people do some strange things for kicks. Take Malaysia's Shahimi Abdul Hamid. In March 2006, he kissed a 15-foot poisonous king cobra 51 times in three minutes. Lucky for him, it didn't bite him once.

FURRY FRIENDS

These must be the bravest bunnies in the world. Of all the animals at a theme park in Sanya, China, that the rabbits could have befriended, they chose tiger cubs. Normally a tiger would view a rabbit as a tasty snack but these artificially bred cubs seem to get along well with their new best buddies, much to the delight of visitors who have flocked to the park to see them. Whether they remain such firm friends when the tigers get bigger is another matter.

HORSE POWER

Is it a bird? Is it a plane? No, it's a horse. For decades, the diving horses were the star attraction on the Steel Pier in Atlantic City, New Jersey. They were trained to walk along a ramp and, sometimes, with a female rider on board, dive 60 feet down into a tank of water. Even though the horses seemed to enjoy it, a number of the riders suffered bad injuries and animal protection societies stopped the show in 1978.

Ripley Replay
June 30, 1989

Andy was born without feet and was taught to walk with the aid of sneakers!

WILD WORLD

MANDRILL GIRLS

With mandrill monkeys, it's a girls-only club. That's what scientists from the Wildlife Conservation Society discovered after spending two years tracking the colorful monkeys in the wilds of Gabon, Africa. The study found that mandrills travel together in enormous groups of between 500 and 1,000 and that these groups are extremely tight-knit. Each member knows all the others—the equivalent of being on a first-name basis with everyone in your school! Even more surprising was the discovery that these packs are made up almost entirely of females and their young. The males join the females only in the mating season, after which they go off to live alone. So the males and females lead virtually separate lives.

NICE TRICK

Penguins perform a neat trick—converting saltwater to freshwater. They do this by means of a special supraorbital gland, located just above the eyes, which functions like a kidney. Living in saltwater environments is a real problem for penguins because saltwater could damage their health. Although they don't drink water, they take it in when they swallow their prey. As a result, saltwater enters their system and must be excreted. This is where this gland comes in. It works in such a way that it strains out any passing saltwater and then swiftly removes the brine from the bird's system through its bill.

Fill 'er Up

The water-holding frog of Australia has found a clever way of adapting to life in the hot, dry desert. It can survive for months and even years in drought conditions. Before the rains stop and the pools dry up, the frog fills up on water, storing it in its bladder and in pockets under its skin. Then using a "spade" on its strong back legs, it burrows backward into the sandy soil to a depth of 8–12 inches. The frog is such a fast digger that it can cover itself in just 30 seconds. Once underground, it seals itself in a transparent waterproof cocoon of loose, shed skin. This hardens around the frog's body, allowing it to hold large amounts of water. And there it stays until the next time there is enough rain to trickle down to its underground hiding place, which could be for as long as two years. Aborigines use the frog as a source of water. They skillfully locate the frog's burrow, place its rear end in their mouth, and squeeze the water from it! Yuk! The good news is that the frog remains unharmed by the experience.

ROARING SUCCESS

An art exhibition was displayed in cages at a Paris zoo! Artist Braco Dimitrijevic spent ten years persuading the French authorities to allow him to put reproductions of famous paintings in the lion house. Bet none of the visitors wanted to get too close to the paintings!

GENTLE GIANT

When a small boy fell into the gorilla pit at an Illinois zoo, a young female helped rescuers by gently carrying him to the workers' door.

PURPLE POLAR

When Pelusa, a polar bear kept in captivity at a zoo in Argentina, developed a skin condition, veterinarians sprayed her with an antiseptic that turned her white fur purple!

PINS AND KNEE-DLES

At the Brookfield Zoo in Illinois, Jewel, a Bactrian camel, suffered such severe arthritis in her front legs that she was almost lame. She was treated successfully with acupuncture!

CREEPY CRAWLIES

It's enough to make your skin crawl! Visitors to Stockholm Zoo in Sweden are allowed to cuddle spiders—under supervision. Would you want a hairy tarantula crawling all over your face?

ODD ONE OUT

Bengal tiger cub Saimai was suckled by a sow and raised with a litter of piglets at a tiger farm in Thailand. The Big Bad Wolf would have got a shock if he had tried eating one of those little pigs!

BEAR NECESSITY

Juan, an Andean spectacled bear, decided he simply had to escape from Germany's Berlin Zoo. After paddling across a moat using a log as a raft and scaling the wall of his enclosure, he tried to make his getaway on a bicycle that he had found leaning on some railings! But before he could climb into the saddle, he was cornered by keepers and taken back to his home.

SLOW MOTION

The Alaska Zoo in Anchorage has installed what is thought to be the world's first elephant treadmill, because their star attraction, 24-year-old Maggie, is a bit lazy and doesn't like to exercise.

MOTHER LOVE

Some moms can be a little too caring, as Reggie, a baby baboon born at Paignton Zoo, England, learned to his cost. Believe It or Not! his mother groomed him so forcefully that she licked all the fur off his head, leaving poor Reggie bald!

PET-ICULAR TALENT

GOOOOOAL!

It might appear to be a hard task teaching elephants to play soccer, but they've succeeded in Thailand. And to mark the 2006 World Cup, the elephants were decorated in national colors to take part in a match against a team of Thai students. What they lack in mobility, the elephants make up for in strength—and of course they never forget the score. But when an elephant dribbles, you wouldn't want to be on the receiving end!

PLANNING OF THE APES

New research shows that apes such as orangutans and bonobos actually prepare for outings, remembering to bring along the tools they will need to get their food. So if you're going on a picnic and forget the can opener, ask a gorilla.

WAVE TO GO!

Twiggy the gray squirrel can do more than just climb trees—she is also an excellent waterskier! Towed at speeds of up to 6 miles an hour by a remote-controlled model boat, Twiggy skis around a mini Manhattan at boat shows across America. She is trained by Lou Ann Best of Sanford, Florida, who says the key to success is affection, patience, and a plentiful supply of squirrel food!

HIGH LIFE

Zoe, a cat from Lake Hughes, California, can walk across two parallel wires suspended 4½ feet in the air—and she hasn't fallen yet. One of her trainers, Rob Bloch, says he taught Zoe to pad the high wire by placing her at one end of the wire and her favorite chicken or beef food at the other. But they don't use turkey because that makes her sleepy. And they wouldn't want Zoe to drop off!

Ripley Replay
April 30, 1972

Rollie the penguin liked skating so much he joined the National Rollerskating Association!

WHO'S YOUR DADDY?

DAZZLING DADS

Female Barbary macaque monkeys of Morocco mate with several males, and no one really knows who is the father of which baby. But that doesn't stop the males from being caring parents. They often snatch the newborn babies from their mothers and take them on outings. Not only do they babysit, they also use the babies to bond with other dads, sometimes offering them as presents when greeting rival males.

PEA-POPS

Peacocks are renowned for their magnificent displays, but as fathers, they're more than just a pretty set of tail feathers. Not only do they guard the nest fiercely, they also help with building it and rearing the chicks. They have even been known to give the chicks a piggyback ride every now and then. What great dads!

CHICK CRÈCHE

There's safety in numbers for emperor chick penguins. When the young birds have grown large enough, the adults often form crèches, grouping a number of chicks together to protect them from predators. A penguin will leave its chick at a crèche while it goes off to fish, as long as a few adults stay behind to look after the youngsters. Penguins just might be the model parents of the natural world.

FIN-TASTIC!

The male bluegill sunfish of America are the nest-builders. After females lay the eggs, the males guard the nest. Once the eggs have hatched, they stay and watch over the young.

Ripley Replay
Circa 1950

Taking parenting to extremes: one dog, many mouths to fill.

MORE THE MERRIER

BIRD'S BURDEN

Colonel Sanders might very well have been pleased to see a chicken discovered in Jiangsu Province, China, in 2005 because it had two extra legs! The mutated bird, which was found among 500 test chickens, had an extra pair of legs hanging from its hips. A four-legged chicken may sound like a novelty but the added limbs restricted the bird's mobility and put it well down the pecking order.

SNAKES ALIVE!

Ten-year-old Hunter York of Centertown, Kentucky, was out walking near his home when he spotted a black king snake, about 8 ½ inches long. As he picked it up with a stick, he noticed the snake grabbed the stick with two heads! The chances of a two-headed snake are one in 10,000.

HEADS START

Think two heads are certainly better than one? Just ask a turtle discovered at a market in Qingdao, China, in March 2005. The animal's owner, Mr Xiao, says that the two heads coordinate very well and can even eat at the same time. Not surprisingly, they eat more than normal one-headed turtles. It's thought that this unique trait occurred as a result of the bodies of a pair of twin turtles failing to separate properly during development.

NO KIDDING!

Farmer Juan Bolanos of Bauta, Cuba, was stunned in 2004 when one of his animals gave birth to a goat that had two heads. Incredibly, the young goat was able to breathe and feed with both heads. It even opened and closed its four eyes at the same time. Unfortunately, the kid didn't survive for very long.

Ripley Replay
April 24, 1935

This lamb, born in Texas, had one head, two bodies, and two front and four back legs.

MISCEL-LOONY-OUS!

STACK MAN

Doug Fishbone piled high an amazing 17,000 bananas in the middle of Washington Street, Brooklyn, in 2002. Why? He liked the way they looked! It cost him nearly $1,700 and took over five hours to arrange the heap that measured about 6 feet high and 10 feet in diameter. When he was bored with it, he invited passersby to help him dismantle it by helping themselves to the fruit. Not surprisingly, some of them thought that Doug was bananas!

COMPLETELY NUTS

Mark McGowan used his nose to push a peanut 7 miles along the streets of London. During his journey he sometimes had to replace the peanut after it fell down a drain or was stepped on by people!

BARELY THERE

The only way to view Chinese painter Jin Yin Hua's 2006 portrait of a giant panda is through a microscope. That's because he painstakingly painted the panda on a single strand of human hair! Naturally, he couldn't use an ordinary brush to paint something so tiny, so he used a single piece of rabbit hair instead. It took him 10 days and a lot of patience to finish his masterpiece!

MEOW!

Bob Martin from Hampshire, England, loved the musical *Cats*. In fact he loved it so much that he traveled to London to watch it every week for 14 years! From 1988 until the show closed in 2002, he spent 90 days and $37,000 traveling 52,000 miles to watch 795 performances. He said he didn't know what he was going to do after it closed. For Bob it was nothing short of a cat-astrophe.

Ripley Replay
October 15, 1931

Tom Breen could write and draw with both hands and feet, together, in four languages!

ENERGY BURST

BANANA BUNCH

A bunch of Australian farmers are looking into the appeal of banana fuel to power their tractors. Wondering what to do with all their rotten bananas, they have converted them into a source of energy. These farmers hope to create full-scale, fruit-fired power stations so that Australian homes can run on banana waste. As for the tractors, you can always tell those that are running on banana fuel, because they keep sliding across the road!

TOTALLY NUTS?

Motorists in the Philippines are being encouraged to run their vehicles on diesel fuel extracted from coconut oil. It may sound like a nutty idea, but it could be the road ahead.

POOCH POOP POWER

Poop in the park may be a thing of the past. In San Francisco they are hoping to harness the power of the horrible, smelly methane gas in doggie doo so it can be used for heating homes and providing electricity. The method has already been tried with cows' poop and now experts want to create power from all kinds of manure, sewerage, and household garbage. And it's causing quite a stink!

GOOD VIBRATIONS

Whether it's because of wind, air conditioning, or passing vehicles, a building's walls and windows vibrate all the time. Masayuki Miyazaki, a researcher at a company in Japan, has started converting these movements into electricity. The amount produced is small, but he hopes that eventually it will be enough to power something like a computer. So one day Microsoft Windows could be powered by real windows.

Ripley Replay
March 24, 1932

What an extraordinary sight! A tree that spouted water was found in Virginia.

65

NOW YOU SEE IT

In some places, ice and snow are becoming almost as useful as bricks and stone. At the Ice and Snow Festival in Harbin in northern China, about 325,000 cubic feet of ice are used each year. There, a million visitors suffer 40 degrees below zero to see everything from mammoth animals to 100-foot buildings that are lit by colored bulbs embedded in the ice.

SAND AND DELIVER

Forget sand castles, think palaces . . . or a trumpeting bull elephant, or a 12-foot Marilyn Monroe! At the sand-sculpting world championships, held annually at different beaches around the world, everything from wild mythical creatures to a whole legion of Roman soldiers can emerge from the beach. First, sculptors shovel sand into one enormous pile. Then, they add water, grab a trowel, kitchen implements, or pieces of wood and start carving! Each sculpture takes hours of painstaking work, but to see the results you have to be lucky. Since no glue is allowed, the sea soon takes each one away.

Can-Demonium

In cities in the U.S. and Canada, "Canstruction" events are staged where architects and engineers compete against each other to see who can build the most spectacular structure—out of cans. Thousands of cans and hours of patience go into the creation of sculptures such as the Empire State Building, King Kong, a mermaid, an alarm clock, old-fashioned gas pumps, and even a hissing cobra. When the exhibition is over, the cans are donated to soup kitchens, day care centers, and homes for the elderly.

Say What?

STAR PARTS

John Reznikoff of Stamford, Connecticut, collects the hair of dead celebrities, including John F. Kennedy, Marilyn Monroe, Elvis Presley, and Abraham Lincoln. When British healer Jack Temple died in 2004, he left behind toenail clippings of his famous clients, including Jerry Hall!

POSTMAN

Stephen Knight of Halstead, England, collects all things associated with the Royal Mail. He has over 60 mailboxes in his garden, but still has to walk down the road to mail a letter.

MAGNETIC ATTRACTION

Louise J. Greenfarb of Las Vegas, Nevada, is strongly attracted to fridge magnets. She has been collecting them for 30 years and now has around 30,000. When she dies, she wants to be buried in her fridge, surrounded by a thousand of her favorite magnets!

PLANE TALK

If you feel ill on an airplane, Nick Vermeulen is the guy to know because he has collected more than 2,000 airline sickbags!

CLEAN CACHE

over the past 40 years, California's Charlie Lester has built up a collection of more than 140 vintage vacuum cleaners, dating from 1905 to 1960.

FLUFF FANATIC

Every day since 1984, Australia's Graham Barker has been collecting lint from his navel. He keeps the ball of fluff in his bathroom to show visitors!

MOUSETRAP MANIA

Germany's Reinhard Hellwig collects mousetraps through the ages. He currently has around 2,500 from all over the world.

MAN OF VISION

Up to his death in 2002, Dr. Hugh Hicks, a dentist from Baltimore, Maryland, collected more than 75,000 light bulbs from different countries around the world.

CRAZY COLLECTORS

People who collect things are called by many names — some as unusual as the objects they collect. For example, did you know that a plangonologist collects dolls, an archtophilist collects teddy bears, a vexillologist collects flags, and a vecturist collects subway tokens?

SWEET SENSATION

This mosque could melt in your mouth. That's because it was made from 551 pounds of chocolate. The detailed model, 14 feet by 8 feet, was displayed at a hotel in Jakarta in September 2006, during the fasting month of Ramadan.

ALTOGETHER NOW!

PART ART

This is a Mona Lisa with byte—a re-creation of Leonardo da Vinci's famous portrait made from hundreds of used computer parts. A group of computer engineers used colored chip sockets and circuits to make this high-tech version of the painting. It took them weeks to complete, but the finished product, titled "Technology Smiling," fascinated visitors when it went on display at an exhibition in Beijing, China, in May 2006.

TASTY!

A group of artists called Mondongo don't work in paints. Instead they create pictures using really unusual materials such as chopsticks, cooked meats, cookies, and even cheese!

KING OF INSECTS

Enrique Ramos spends weeks at a time searching old buildings in his native Mexico…for spiderwebs. And it's all in the name of art. When he's found enough, he removes any insects and other living creatures before washing the web, flattening it, stretching it, and leaving it to dry. Then he is ready to use it as a canvas for his unique re-creations of the painting, "The Last Supper," Elvis, and, of course, Spider-Man.

CANDY KING

Here's Dean Cain as you've never seen him before, made from 17,000 gumballs by candy-loving artist Franz Spohn of Pennsylvania. Franz first came up with the idea for candy art after buying some Swedish Fish candies. He didn't like the taste, but didn't want the candy to go to waste, so he made a picture by squishing them between two pieces of glass. Then, he moved on to cupcake sprinkles before discovering gumballs. As well as Dean, he has done incredible gumball portraits of Roy Rogers and Robert Ripley.

Ripley Replay
Late 1970s

Reg Pollard constructed London's Tower Bridge out of matchsticks in his living room!

73

6

ON THE FRINGE

ANIMAL CRACKERS

BUGGIN'

There's something pretty creepy about Kanjana Kaetkeow from Thailand. She once spent 32 days in a plastic cage with 3,400 scorpions, allowing them to crawl all over her body. Happily, unlike the scorpions, the story doesn't have a sting in the tail because in 2006 she got married…to a man who had recently spent 28 days in a cage with 1,000 centipedes. Scorpions and centipedes were even invited to the wedding!

RARELY RATTLED

Jackie Bibby of Texas once sat in a bathtub with 81 rattlesnakes. Another time he shared a sleeping bag with 109 rattlesnakes. And in 37 years of handling rattlers, he has only received eight serious bites.

SNAKE CHARMING

If you want to perform a party trick, you might balance books on your head or juggle. But a guy from India has a trick that nobody can match—he puts his pet snake up his nose and then pulls it out through his mouth. Yuk! It's gross enough when people do it with spaghetti, but with a snake it's really spooky. Bet he wouldn't try it with a python!

BUZZ-ERK

This man is covering himself with hundreds of live honeybees in the hope that they sting him! Muntoyib is a bee-sting therapist from Indonesia, and in January 2006 he undertook this bee-wildering exercise at Jakarta. It was all part of his research into using the venom from live stinging bees to treat chronic pain. So there is a medical explanation for his rather bizarre behavior. Or maybe it's just that he gets a buzz from it!

Ripley Replay
February 9, 1931

Can you find the duck in this picture?

BEYOND BELIEF!

THE LAST STRAW

You won't hurt Marco Hort's feelings by calling him a big mouth — he might even consider it a compliment! The Swiss native is a straw-stuffing specialist. In 2006, he managed to cram 264 straws into his mouth, besting his previous record of 259 straws. In order to achieve this amazing feat, Marco must dislocate his entire jaw. Ouch!

EASY DOES IT!

Ashrita Furman of New York City specializes in performing amazing feats. One of his craziest was in 2004 when he balanced 75 beer glasses on his chin in the backyard of his home in Queens.

KINGPIN

How did you choose to celebrate 2003? Maybe by running 2,003 feet? Well, Wei Shengchu of Nanking, China, marked the year by sticking 2,003 needles in his head! Using a pair of forceps and several containers of ³/₄ inch acupuncture needles, the 53-year-old transformed his head into a pincushion.

BREAKING NEWS!

You wouldn't want to mess with Zoltan Vatkai! In August 2000, the Hungarian strong man and karate expert broke one ton of concrete panels with a single blow. Vatkai, who performed the fearless feat during a demonstration of extreme sports in a parking lot in downtown Budapest, was not injured. In fact, he had a smashing time and emerged in much better shape than the concrete panels. You've got to hand it to him!

Ripley Replay
September 2, 1934

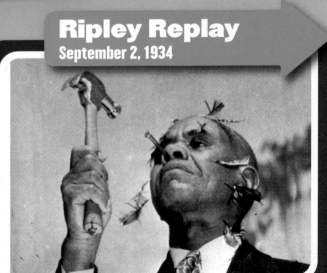

The extraordinary Professor Kongee of Pittsburgh drove 6-inch nails into his nose!

EATING OUTRAGE

TINY TREAT

What was surely the world's smallest Christmas dinner was put up for sale on eBay. The plate measured 2 in by 1 in and held baby carrots, green beans, boiled potatoes, roast potatoes and sausage, and bacon rolls. The seller from Bournemouth, England, said: "I thought it might suit somebody who wanted to watch their weight at Christmas." Although the meal wasn't actually edible, it sold for just over $40...and that included a free, very tiny, Christmas pudding.

LOCUST LUNCH

A lot of you have probably eaten chicken wings. Well, how about eating locust wings? On the last day of a science festival held in Wageningen, the Netherlands, in September 2006, cooks from all over the world gathered to prepare tasty dishes...of insects. Locusts, crickets, maggots, and mealworms were eagerly devoured as visitors tucked into their grub with such enthusiasm that 1,747 portions were eaten. It really was lunch with a crunch.

Sitting Pretty

You may think you have wandered into the wrong room when you visit a new restaurant in Shenzhen, China. For diners sit on glass-covered toilet bowls at toilet-style tables and eat from toilet-shaped platters. The entire restaurant is toilet themed, from the two big toilets sitting at the entrance to the colorful toilet bowls that hang from the walls and serve as light fittings. Even the food is designed to resemble manure...but thankfully only in appearance. Soft chocolate ice cream whipped into a whirl and served in a china potty is definitely not for the squeamish. But the owner, Mr. Lin, is flushed with success. The restaurant has become one of the warmest seats in town, with a waiting list of customers, mainly young people. He had the idea after visiting a toilet exhibition in Paris. In fact his toilet restaurant has done so well that he has now opened up several others.

KNOW YOUR KNOTS!

BOXING CLEVER

A contortionist found himself in a tight corner when he amazingly squeezed his entire body into a small box about the size of a microwave oven. He did it during halftime in the basketball game between the Utah Jazz and the Dallas Mavericks in Salt Lake City in March 2006. And if getting in was tough, getting out wasn't a whole lot easier.

BENDY BOY

Known as The Rubberboy, Los Angeles contortionist Daniel Browning Smith is so flexible that he can disconnect both arms, both legs, and turn his torso 180 degrees.

TIGHT SQUEEZE

Captain Frodo, a contortionist from Norway, can twist his whole body—legs and all—through an unstrung racket. Frodo, who can also squeeze through a wire coat hanger, performs these fantastic feats thanks to a rare genetic condition that enables him to dislocate certain bones in his body. But even he needed practice: one of the first times he attempted the tennis racket trick, he got stuck and needed to be cut free!

Ripley Replay
September 6, 1942

At the age of 14, Bonnie Nebelong's flexibility enabled her to perform amazing handstands!

FUZZY THINKING

HAIR RAISING

When she was 13 in 1973, Xie Qiuping of China decided to grow her hair. After 31 years of continuous growth, it measured 18 feet 5 inches long—that's the height of three tall men!

LONG REACH

Shridhar Chillal of Poona, India, was never tempted to bite his nails—or cut them. Instead, he let the nails on his left hand grow and grow for 48 years until, by 1998, their combined length was an incredible 20 feet 2 inches. Shridhar, who says he was inspired by the deeds of a Chinese priest, doesn't grow the nails on his right hand, which at least means he's got one hand free for doing things like opening doors or washing his face.

FANCY GRILLEWORK

When rap star Paul Wall smiles, it's hard not to notice. That's because he has one of America's most expensive smiles—a $25,000 grin that flashes the array of dazzling jewelry on his teeth. Wall's is one of the world's glitziest grilles—the name given to the trend for gold, platinum, and diamond-encrusted teeth. He even has his own store in Houston, Texas, that supplies customized grilles to hip-hop stars and other entertainers.

Ripley Replay
1950s

How did she work that hairdo with those nails?

STUCK UP!

Matt Robison of Ottawa, Canada, spent 14 hours on March 18, 2006, having 1,016 piercings inserted into the flesh on his arms and back. He complained that having so many body piercings in one sitting was painful, not to mention really exhausting! As soon as he reached his target, he began to remove them all—which was every bit as painful as putting them in.

Fear Facts

TRAIN OF THOUGHT

Sigmund Freud, the famous Austrian who pioneered the study of dreams and the unconscious mind, suffered from siderodromophobia, a fear of train travel.

SPOOKY OR WHAT?

American actress Natalie Wood suffered from hydrophobia, a fear of water. She died in 1981 by drowning.

SIMPLY POTTY

Antonia Hart of South Africa claims to have developed a phobia about toilets after falling off one at a hotel in 2003!

FROZEN IN FEAR

Louise Arnold of Bishop's Cleeve, England, has such a severe phobia of peas that it has caused her to flee restaurants and avoid the frozen food aisle in supermarkets!

JAWS ALERT

Did you know? Some people suffer from selachophobia—an irrational fear of sharks. Some sufferers fear is so great that they are unable to swim even in a pool.

SHOT FLEAS

Queen Christina of Sweden (1626-1689) had a phobia about fleas. She was terrified of them and ordered a tiny cannon just 4 inches long to be built so that she could fire miniature cannonballs at the fleas!

FUNNY FEELING

Coulrophobia is the fear of clowns. Sufferers say the cause is the clown's heavy makeup, bulbous nose, and weird hair color that conceal the wearer's identity. This phobia is more common than you think—a number of websites have been set up to address the condition.

CLEAN LIVING

Actress Katharine Hepburn had a phobia about dirty hair. When she was at Twentieth Century Fox, she used to tour the movie set sniffing people's hair to make sure that it had been washed.

UNLUCKY NUMBER

Triskaidekaphobia is the fear of the number 13. That's why houses in some streets don't have a number 13 and why most hotels in Las Vegas don't have a 13th floor. Composer Arnold Schoenberg suffered from this phobia. He was born — and eventually died — on the 13th of the month and dreaded turning 76 because its digits add up to 13. And he wouldn't give any of his operas titles with 13 letters.

7

RISKY BUSINESS!

ALL FALL DOWN

BIG CHILL

When his plane skidded into a lake in Alaska in December 2003, pilot Wade Strahan survived 24 hours in sub-freezing temperatures. A pilot with more than 30 years of experience, Strahan was planning a sightseeing flight over the Chugach Mountains. But instead, as he tried to take off from a remote airfield, his Cessna C-172 was unable to get airborne and skidded about 100 feet into Eklutna Lake, some 40 miles northeast of Anchorage. After swimming ashore, Strahan battled the icy conditions and hiked to a trapper's cabin, even though his shoes were frozen to his feet. He spent the bitterly cold night in the unheated cabin and still had the strength to hike 8 miles the next day to a spot where he was found by cross-country skiers.

FLYING BLIND

Over 300 passengers on board a flight from Canada to Portugal had an incredible escape after the pilot landed the plane without any engines or brakes on a tiny island in the Atlantic Ocean. Canadian Transat Flight 236 from Toronto to Lisbon on August 24, 2001 was uneventful until both engines suddenly failed. As the plane started to lose altitude, Pilot Robert Piché was guided by controllers to the island of Terceira, but, with a haze below, he couldn't see the airport runway. When he finally saw it lit up by emergency vehicles, he was approaching too fast, too high, and with no brakes. On impact tires blew, sparks flew, the plane jerked alarmingly from side to side, but miraculously came to a halt.

Taking A Dive

When both the parachute and back-up parachute of Shayna Richardson of Joplin, Missouri, failed, she fell 10,000 feet face-first into an asphalt parking lot—and survived! On October 9, 2005, she prepared to make her tenth jump—but her first solo jump—above Siloam Springs. Shayna knew she was in trouble when she heard a snap and started spinning. So she tried to open her reserve 'chute, but that, too, failed to open—a chance of one in a million.

As she plunged toward the ground, she felt sure she was going to die. She lived to tell the tale, but her biggest shock was still to come. While she was in the emergency room, she was surprised to learn that she was two weeks pregnant. Amazingly, in June 2006 she gave birth to a healthy boy, Tanner, who appears not to have been affected by the accident that left his mom with 15 steel plates in her face. So has Shayna, seen here with her instructor, given up skydiving? Nope! She said that one of the first things she was going to do once the baby was born was go skydiving again!

IT'S A CAR'S LIFE!

RIDING HIGH

Suspending a car in midair... it looks like one of David Copperfield's fantastic illusions! But in fact it's the result of a car delivery truck driving under a low bridge in Britain. The driver of the transporter forgot how low the bridge was when he attempted to pass under it, and one of the vehicles on the top deck became wedged beneath the bridge. There it stayed until the emergency services hauled it down to the ground. You can bet he didn't make the same mistake again!

SMASHING!

The newly opened Car Crash Restaurant in Santiago, Chile, was closed in July 2005, after a car skidded on the wet road and crashed into the building!

UNWELCOME VISITOR

Frank and Jacqueline Tuttle were sitting in the front room of their house in Norwich, England, when an out-of-control car crashed through the window. The room was destroyed in a cloud of dust and rubble. "There was no warning," says Mr. Tuttle. "Just an almighty crash. Although my wife suffered a bad leg injury, we count ourselves lucky. If the car had come through five minutes later, my daughter would have been sitting there."

EYE-CATCHING

Watching Li Chuanyong in action always manages to cause a few raised eyebrows…or raised eyelids! In March 2006, using only his eyelids, he pulled a wagon containing seven beauty pageant winners and an 880-pound stone cauldron, a total weight of around three tons, along a street in Xingan City, China. He also uses his eyelids to lift pails of water. The most puzzling thing about his unusual talent is, how did he find out he was good at it?

Ripley Replay
March 17, 1985

Oliver Albert of Gonzales, Texas, built this Longhorn V-12 from 14 different makes of cars.

Against the Odds

CRUSHED CAR

In the aftermath of the Los Angeles earthquake of 1994, a man known only as Salvador was trapped in a car, crushed under the weight of hundreds of tons of concrete blocks and twisted steel. For six hours, he was kept alive with air pumped from a compressor into his mangled vehicle before rescuers could finally reach him.

MAKESHIFT RAFT

A 2004 tsunami killed thousands of people in Indonesia. Rizal Shahputra survived at sea by clinging to tree branches. He subsisted on rainwater and coconuts for eight days.

A MIRACLE!

Eight days after the city of Bam was destroyed by the 2004 Iranian earthquake, rescuers had given up finding any more survivors. Then, Shahrbanou Mazandarani, aged 90, was found! She had been saved by a piece of wood that had toppled over and protected her.

SAFEST PLACE

The 1902 eruption of Mont Pelée on Martinique, a Caribbean island, killed everybody in the town of St. Pierre—except two people. One of the lucky survivors was a prisoner being held in a thick-walled cell.

PEAK PLUNGE

Ed Maginn from Utah escaped with only minor injuries after tumbling a vertical half-mile down Alaska's Mount Mckinley in 2006. He fell and tumbled 2,600 feet down a steep snow gully while making a skiing turn.

BADLY BURNED

Lauren Manning was in Tower 1 of the World Trade Center when the first plane struck on September 11, 2001. Engulfed by a huge ball of fire, she suffered burns to more than 80 percent of her body. She pulled through and is making a full recovery.

JUST IN TIME

In September 1993, The Sunset Limited train crashed, exploded, and plunged into an alligator-infested creek near Mobile, Alabama. Forty-seven people were killed, but as her train car rapidly filled with water, Elizabeth Watts managed to escape.

MIRACULOUS SURVIVAL

After a landslide hit a ski resort at Thredbo, Australia, in 1997, rescuers had been digging through rubble for three days before they discovered Stuart Diver. He survived because he had been trapped in the empty space between two slabs of concrete.

RUBBLE RESCUE

Four people were rescued after being trapped for ten days in the rubble of a building in the Philippines town of Real in 2004. They had survived by drinking water that was dripping from the ceiling of the building, which had been destroyed by a typhoon.

PYTHON PLAYMATE

A three-year-old Cambodian boy has an unusual best friend—a 13 foot-long female python named Lucky! Villagers have flocked to see the boy, Oeun Sambat, who they believe has supernatural powers and was the son of a dragon in a former life.

WHALE OF A TIME!

Champion free diver Tanya Streeter can hold her breath under water for six minutes. As she doesn't need to carry scary-looking air bottles, marine animals treat her like a strange fish. They allow her to swim and play with them. In this way she has been able to make close contact with humpback whales, sharks, marine iguanas, turtles, sea lions, manatees, and penguins. Humpback whales have even been known to flirt with her!

BRRR-AVE MAN

Standing around for four hours might not sound very daring but 48-year-old Jin Songhao from northern China did it in freezing temperatures of minus 29°C and without any clothes on!

GOLF NUTS

Your eyes aren't deceiving you: these people are playing golf on a giant chessboard. It's one of the spray-painted holes designed to add a little fun and color to the Lucifer's Anvil course in the middle of Nevada's Black Rock Desert. You've got to be crazy to play there. The course is over such a vast area that, in the annual tournament, competitors travel around on mountain bikes, and putts of 150 yards are commonplace.

THE HIGH LIFE

Known as Spiderman, daredevil Frenchman Alain Robert scales tall buildings without any safety devices—just his bare hands and climbing shoes. He has climbed over 70 large structures, including the 110-story Sears Tower in Chicago, and has fallen seven times but he keeps bouncing back.

Ripley Replay
January 12, 1937

Daniel Vilizio from Pennsylvania pulls along his brother while skating on his hands.

8

MAD SCIENCE

PHARMA-ZOO-TICALS

HISSY CURE

Most people keep well away from rattlesnakes, but some snake venom may be healthy for you. A drug used to treat acute heart disease is actually derived from the venom of the Southeastern pygmy rattlesnake.

DOC PYTHON

Few people can afford modern medicines in Cambodia, where over a third of the population lives on under $1 a day. Instead, they place great faith in the supernatural healing powers of animals such as cows, turtles, and snakes. One such creature is an albino python, whose blessing is believed to cure ailments.

WORTH SPIT

A drug called exenatide is being used to help type 2 diabetics who don't respond to insulin. It might promote weight loss. Where does this new wonder drug come from? It's a synthetic version of a protein derived from the saliva of the Gila monster, found in North and Central America and one of only two venomous lizards in the world. So while a bite from a Gila monster may be dangerous, the lizard could also be good news for diabetics.

THAT'S A LEAP!

If you want to avoid getting bitten by mosquitoes, the answer could be to carry around an Australian dumpy tree frog. The sweat of this frog has proved to be an effective mosquito repellent! Researchers from the University of Adelaide smeared the frog's secretion over the hairless tail of a mouse kept in a cage with 80 mosquitoes. Other mice were bitten instantly, but the insects stayed well away from the treated tail.

Ripley Replay
July 6, 1933

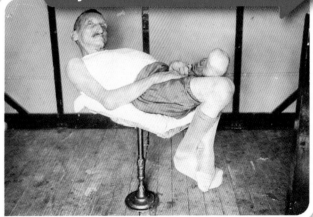

Harry Overduff's body started turning to stone. Eventually he was unable to move.

Brave New World

WINGED WONDERS

Scientists in Britain are creating robot flies that could be sent to locate victims of natural disasters such as earthquakes. They hope the tiny machine insects could operate in confined spaces where humans are unable to go.

BACK TO THE FUTURE

Scientists plan to use bits of DNA encased in the bone marrow and muscle of a prehistoric woolly mammoth that was recovered from the Siberian tundra to clone this huge prehistoric beast.

IN THE BLINK OF AN EYE

Airports may soon be using machines that automatically scan the iris area of the eye, compare it to a database of images, and thus identify people.

BRIGHT IDEA

University students in Singapore have injected a plant with jellyfish DNA so that it glows whenever it needs to be watered!

SAY CHEESE!

At the University of California, scientists have created an artificial insect eye containing 8,500 hexagonal lenses in an area the size of a pinhead! It is hoped that the artificial eye could one day be used in ultra-thin cameras.

TOUCHY FEELY

American scientists have developed a robotic sensor that can "feel" to the same degree of sensitivity as a human fingertip. The device is so sensitive that when a penny was pressed against it, the sensor detected the wrinkles in President Lincoln's clothing and the letters "T" and "Y" in liberty!

STEPPING OUT

In Japan, they have manufactured a robotic dance partner. The robot's memory holds the dance steps and can also sense pressure in its arms and back to stay in time with its human partner.

CRUMB OF COMFORT

People have been baffled as to why toast seems to land butter-side down. Now scientists have discovered that it's all in the way you spread it. Apparently, if you press firmly and quickly with the knife as you spread, it creates a dip in the toast that causes it to land with the curved sides up instead.

MIND READERS

Scientists have had success mapping brains to discover why different people are better at different jobs. For example, when shown a variety of images, the brains of extroverts light up in different areas than the brains of introverts. Some employment agencies are thinking about using brain scans as a hiring tool!

GAG-A-LICIOUS!

STICK IT

If you think superglue is strong, it's nothing compared to the glue that is produced by a microscopic bacterium called *Caulobacter crescentus*. Scientists have found that it manages to cling to the inside of water pipes with the strongest glue known to exist. Incredibly the bacteria stay in place on the pipe's surface because they can withstand a force equivalent to five tons per square inch. And that is really powerful. The glue, which is produced at the tips of the stalks of the bacteria's cells, is so minute that its average diameter is 250 times thinner than a human hair! Who knows, we might end up mending broken toys and ornaments with glue from an organism that is invisible to the naked eye!

BACON AND WORMS?

Bacon has never been recommended by medical experts as a particularly healthy thing to eat, but all that could now be changing. Omega-3 fatty acids that are found in fish and some grains are very healthy for humans because they are thought to combat heart disease. Scientists have found that a tiny roundworm also manufactures Omega-3s, and geneticists led by Dr. Jing Kang, a Harvard Medical School researcher, decided to try and use advanced DNA techniques to mix the worm's genes with that of pigs. After he had modified the omega-3-making worm gene, his colleagues found a way of adding it to pigs, the result being swine that produce significant amounts of omega-3s. So it could be that in years to come bacon will be just as healthy for you as fish or granola.

Yellow Cure

A few hundred years ago there were all kinds of strange medical cures. People believed that carrying a child through a flock of sheep would cure breathing problems, that carrying a dead shrew in your pocket would ward off rheumatism, and that throwing a dung beetle over your shoulder would cure stomachache. But not all of these beliefs have died out. Today, people in India are being encouraged to drink cow urine as a cure for a variety of ailments. The healing properties of cow dung and cow urine are mentioned in ancient Hindu texts, and now research by doctors apparently suggests that the urine can cure anything from skin diseases and kidney and liver ailments to obesity and heart conditions. The urine is collected every day from almost 600 shelters for rescued and wounded cattle in the Gujarat region and is sold for 30 pence a bottle under the label "Gift of the Cow." It also comes in tablet form or as a cream mixed with other traditional medicinal herbs. Although many doctors are highly skeptical about the cure, Vidhyaben Mehta, a 65-year-old woman with a cancerous tumour, has been taking cow's urine for the past three years and despite predictions that she would die, says she is no longer in pain.

EYE DROPS

This Chinese stunt man can squirt milk through his eye by blowing hard against his blocked nose! He sucks the milk up his nostrils and then squirts it through his tear ducts.

X-TREME ANATOMY

LITTLE BIG MAN

At 14 years old, Khagendra Thapa is just 20 inches tall and weighs less than 10 pounds—the same weight as a healthy baby. His mother believes the reason he is so small is that he only started moving when he was eight and his physical growth stopped three years later. Although he is small, Khagendra loves playing and singing.

HIGH LIFE

For Xi Shun, finding clothes that fit is a tall order. That's because, at 7 feet 9 inches, he needs pants with extra, extra, extra long legs. Not surprisingly, he has them specially made. His house in Mongolia was also built to suit his requirements and contains a king-size bed measuring 8 feet 6 inches long. Amazingly, Xi Shun was just like any other boy until he was 16. In his teenage years, Xi Shun suddenly had a growth spurt, which carried on and on for seven years. He now leads a quiet life as a herdsman.

Hair Attack

This unnamed Mexican boy suffers from hypertrichosis, the condition which means "extra hair." It is also known as werewolf syndrome because it leaves people looking like mythical werewolves. In the most extreme cases, the face, torso, arms and legs are all covered in hair. The only parts of the skin that remain hairless are the palms of hands and soles of feet. Luckily, it is a very rare disorder, and only 19 people alive today have hypertrichosis. The chances of it happening are 10 billion to one. It is therefore not surprising that only 50 cases have been recorded since the Middle Ages. Many of those diagnosed have turned the situation to their advantage by starring in circuses and sideshows. The most famous of all is Manuel Aceves of Mexico, who became known as the Wolf Man. Twenty-four members of Manuel's family have suffered from this disorder, and some have followed him into the circus. However, his great-nephew, Jesus Aceves, decided to shave his face so that he could work in a hotel, while his sister, Lillia, who works for the police in Mexico, sports a full beard!

MEDICAL WONDERS

NAILED!

When an Oregon man went to the hospital complaining of a headache, doctors were surprised to see X-rays showed 12 nails embedded in his skull. Although all of the nails were close to major blood vessels and the brain stem, the man made a full recovery.

KNIFED!

An eight-inch serrated knife was removed from the head of 41-year-old Michael Hill in Jacksonville, Florida, in 1998. After the attack, he walked down the street to a friend's house—with the knife still embedded in his skull. He was then taken to hospital where, lying on a stretcher, he tried to remove the blade himself but was stopped by nurses. Amazingly the next day following surgery he was functioning normally and, despite memory loss and paralysis to his left hand, he was well enough to leave the hospital a week later.

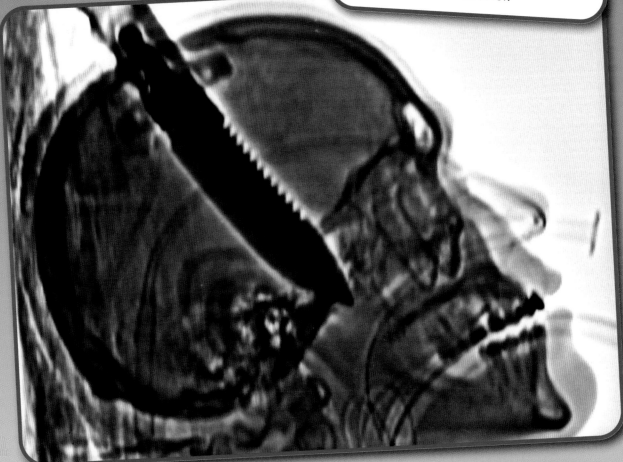

FACE TIME

Isabelle Dinoire of Amiens, France, received a face transplant from a dead woman after her own was disfigured by a dog attack. A 15-hour operation left her with just a faint scar around her nose, mouth, and chin where surgeons stitched on a mask of tissue from the donor. Although she has complete feeling in the new tissue, she admits she still gets a shock when she looks at photos and compares her new face with her old one.

OPERATION ZERO

Performing an intricate operation was the least of the surgeons' problems when they operated for the first time under zero gravity over southwestern France in September 2006. During the first operation, the surgeons from Bordeaux University battled hard to keep their feet on the ground. Team members watched them work, floating aboard a plane free-falling to create weightless conditions. The reason? To have a trial run for surgery on astronauts in space.

Ripley Replay
July 12, 1932

W. V. Meadows, shot in the eye in a battle in 1863, coughed up the bullet 58 years later!

9 SPOOKY TALES

OUT OF THIS WORLD

1947 Kenneth Arnold sights nine UFOs near Mt Rainer, Washington State.

1947 A UFO supposedly crashes at Roswell, New Mexico.

1948 Pilot Thomas Mantell crashes while chasing a UFO near Fort Knox, Kentucky.

1948 Pilot George Gorman has a "dogfight" with a UFO at Fargo, North Dakota.

1961 Betty and Barney Hill claim to have been abducted by aliens near Indian Head, New Hampshire.

1964 An alien craft apparently lands at Alamogordo, New Mexico.

1973 Charles Hickson and Calvin Parker claim to have been abducted and taken aboard a UFO while fishing at Pascagoula, Mississippi.

1973 Four army reservists in a helicopter confront a UFO near Mansfield, Ohio.

1997 Mysterious lights appear over Phoenix, Arizona.

MAN OR MOTH?

Between 1966 and 1977, a strange creature called Mothman was repeatedly sighted around Point Pleasant, West Virginia. It was described as a man-sized beast with wings and large reflective red eyes. So was it a man, a moth, or a myth?

116

A CLOSE ENCOUNTER?

Could this be evidence of the existence of UFOs? Pilot David Hastings from Norwich, England, certainly thinks so. He and his co-pilot were flying over California's Mojave Desert in 2000 when a mystery black shape approached them head-on, then flashed overhead. Seconds later, they realized an object was moving alongside them at high speed. Convinced they had encountered a UFO, Hastings took photos and showed them to the U.S. Navy. The incident remains shrouded in mystery.

ALIEN LANDING

Bob Tohak has believed in UFOs since he was a kid. He is so eager to make contact with aliens that he has erected a 42-foot-high UFO landing port on his property in Poland, Wisconsin. The steel platform can support the weight of a helicopter—or a flying saucer. He hopes to install two big light boards and music too.

Ripley Replay
1989

This unidentified UFO was photographed flying above Russia.

THAT'S THE SPIRIT

BUMPS IN THE NIGHT

One night in 1977, the Harper children of Enfield, England, were lying in bed when strange things started to happen in their house. There were knocking sounds on walls, beds jumping up and down, toy bricks flying through the air, furniture mysteriously moving. The children were also levitated off their beds. These spooky spells continued for two years before they stopped as suddenly as they had started. Was it a poltergeist at work, or were the girls just playing games?

HAUNTED HOUND

The Whaley House in San Diego, California, is reputed to be the most haunted house in the United States. It has five human ghosts plus one of a dog that has been seen running down the hall and into the dining room.

WHALE OF A TALE

Could there be a creepy crew aboard a ghost ship? Visitors to the *Charles W. Morgan*, a 166-year-old wooden whaling boat, say it is haunted by its old crew members. People have reported seeing men in nineteenth-century clothing working below deck even when the ship is supposed to be deserted. Others have heard groans and creaking and have felt sickness and death in the air. And where can you find this ship? Appropriately enough, in Mystic, Connecticut!

NO ARM IN IT

Look closely at the picture of Robert A. Ferguson addressing a spiritual convention in Los Angeles in 1968. It appears perfectly normal, except that the shape next to Ferguson is said to be his dead brother Walter, who was killed in 1944. Robert Ferguson claimed that the arm and hand held forward did not belong to either him or Walter! How spooky is that?

Ripley Replay
March 20, 1930

A bolt of lightning killed this man. Two of his gravestones were also destroyed by lightning!

Goosebumps

CREEPY QUILT

When a woman moved into a house in Wisconsin, she found a haunted quilt! People who slept under it claimed that it talked to them, tugged itself off the bed, and even crawled under furniture!

SCHOOL'S OUT!

Kids in Malaysia have found a good excuse for not going to their school—they claim it is haunted by a headless ghost. Students have been scared away from attending classes at Senawang Secondary School, where the figure has been seen in the library, canteen, and toilets in broad daylight.

TROUBLED SOLE

A shop in Cornwall, England, called in a vicar to exorcise a ghost who had become obsessed with a pair of brown shoes! Shop workers said the shoes kept moving around and jumping off shelves.

LETTERS FROM THE DEAD

Two letters said to be dictated by a ghost helped acquit a woman of murder in Brazil. The letters, written by a medium who claimed they were from the dead man, were used as evidence for the defense. The spirit stated that the accused was innocent, and the jury believed him.

SUBWAY SPOOK

Since the 1950s, a tall man dressed in evening wear has reputedly haunted Covent Garden subway station in London, England. When approached, the ghost disappears immediately.

120

AAGH-RIA

The Woodstock Opera House in Illinois is believed to be haunted by the ghost of Elvira, an actress who died there. Apparently she likes seat number 113, and witnesses say they have seen the seat lower mysteriously by itself.

At least three U.S. Presidents, one First Lady, and one visiting European monarch claim to have seen the ghost of Abraham Lincoln walking around the White House.

GHOST FOR SALE

In 2004, the ghost of Indiana's Collin Proctor, in the form of his walking cane, was sold on eBay for $65,000! Mary Anderson put her father's ghost up for sale to help her young son handle his grandfather's death. She even asked the buyer to write to the boy acknowledging receipt of the ghost.

EVIL SPIRIT

A village council in India has fined two brothers for keeping a pet ghost! An exorcist summoned by villagers stated that the pet ghost was responsible for an outbreak of disease in the area. The brothers were fined $700.

GHOUL POWER

All sorts of spooky ghouls and mummies inhabit Michel Dircken's house in Brussels, Belgium—but they're all made from household waste and other recycled materials. His fantasy art museum is a favorite with visitors . . . especially on Halloween.

GRAVE NEWS

DEAD SCARY

More than six million people are buried in underground chambers beneath the city of Paris, France. The network of caves and grottos, known as catacombs, is located in what were once Roman limestone quarries. Near the end of the eighteenth century these quarries were converted into a mass tomb. In the nineteenth century some poor people even lived in the catacombs, next to the skulls and skeletons!

IN LOVING MEMORY

As a memento of someone you love who has died, you can now wear the ashes of their cremated remains in a necklace. LifeGem, in the U.S.A., uses super-hot ovens to transform the ashes to graphite and then presses the stone into blue and yellow diamonds that sell for between $2,700 and $25,000. The procedure can even be undertaken with pets.

PET CEMETERY

A pet cemetery in Tokyo, Japan, has more than 4,000 individual memorials containing the ashes of deceased pets. These owners spend small fortunes on their cherished cats and dogs. An enormous pet cemetery can also be found in Paris, France. It is a final resting home for dogs, including movie star Rin Tin Tin, horses, monkeys, lions, and even fish! But if visiting a burial site is too time-consuming, poems about that special rabbit, frog or parrot, even a photo, can be recorded on some of the virtual pet cemeteries on the Internet.

Ground Dog Days

In 1896, a veterinarian, Dr. Samuel Johnson, offered his apple orchard in Hartsdale, New York, as a burial plot for a friend's dog. Now 70,000 pets are buried there.

Ripley Replay
December, 1929

NERO
AN AIREDALE
BORN 14 DAYS
BEFORE JAN.12.1918
DIED DEC.19.1929
KILLED 10,000 RATS
A
"DOG GONE"
GOOD
DOG GONE

Nero, one man's best friend.

FREAKY FUN!

ROCKY INFORMATION

Archaeologists in Norfolk, England, became very excited when crude carvings of fire, serpents, and a dragon were found on some rocks. They estimated the carvings to be 2,000 years old . . . until a local man admitted he had done them just eight years earlier!

WISH YOU WERE HERE

After the 5-foot-tall inflatable snowman, known as Frosty, was stolen outside his home in Wales, his owner received postcards from him that were sent from all over the world! Helen Bevan had postcards from Tenerife, Antigua, Mexico, Malaysia, Thailand, and Hong Kong, each signed with the words "All my love, Frosty." In them he complained about the heat and told of his travels. Mrs. Bevan thought it was funny, but for the kidnapped Frosty it was snow joke!

FUNNY BUNNY

If you go to one mountain in northern Italy, you'll never believe your eyes. For on the side of the 5,000-feet Colletto Fava mountain lies a giant pink bunny! The 200-foot-long rabbit, knitted over 5 years by an army of old ladies, was put there by a group of Austrian artists to put a smile on people's faces and to make them feel small, like in *Gulliver's Travels*. But the artists say it's not just for laughing at—they expect hikers to climb its 20-foot sides, relax on its belly, and wince at the fake entrails that spew from a wound on the rabbit's side.

NEVERMORE!

According to legend, England will fall unless at least six ravens are left at the Tower of London. So the people in charge take no chances. To stop the birds from flying away, their wings are clipped. There are always seven ravens at the tower— the required six, plus a spare.

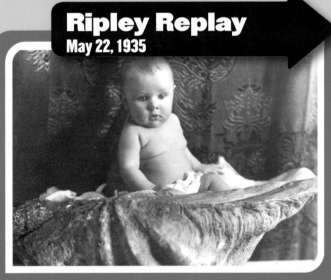

Ripley Replay
May 22, 1935

A clam baby bath! This massive South Seas shell measures 35 inches by 21 inches.

10

BELIEVE IT!

WHAT'S NEW?

TOWER POWER

It looks like the world's craziest parking garage, but in fact it's a storage tower for new cars in Wolfsburg, Germany. Hundreds of cars are lifted hydraulically into their positions in the 20-story cylindrical towers at Volkswagen's Autostadt theme park. When you come to collect your new car, the vehicle is automatically lowered from its place in the tower to the car distribution center—just like a candy vending machine.

NO STRINGS

Scientists have created a T-shirt that allows air guitarists to play actual music. The top has special devices built into its elbows that pick up the player's movements and relay them to a computer, which then interprets them as guitar sounds.

DRESSED TO TRILL

What does every well-dressed bird need for a night out? Answer: a diaper. Mark and Lorraine Moore, concerned for the way their pet birds left their mark in the living room when let out from their cages, invented the bird diaper as a means of allowing birds to live in the home outside a cage. The free fliers now can pick from a variety of colors, sizes, and designs, and ruffle a few feathers with their new look.

SMELLY VISIONS

In some Japanese movie theaters, not only can you watch a movie, you can also smell it! A company has mixed herbs and oils to create aromas that are supposed to heighten the drama during certain scenes. Seven different fragrances wafted from machines under the seats during *The New World*, starring Colin Farrell. A floral smell accompanied love scenes, with a combination of peppermint and rosemary for those tear-jerking moments. Lucky there were no scenes involving beans!

Ripley Replay
1960s

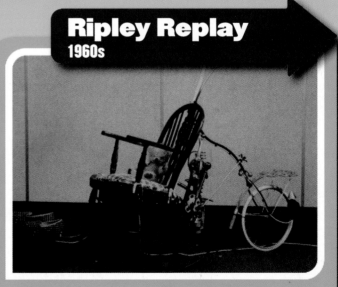

Rowland Emett of England made this chair, rocked by a hot-air engine.

GOOD TO GO

PLAYING AROUND

The craze for customizing cars began in the 1960s when rock stars like John Lennon and Janis Joplin had their cars painted in bright patterns. Now cars show up at festivals covered in such items as dolls, stone, brick, cork, pennies, grass, plaid, and tree bark. Harrod Blank's Pico de Gallo is a Volkswagen Bug covered in records and musical instruments. It should be easy to tune the engine!

POLISHED!

Yvonne Miller from South Carolina used more than 100 bottles of nail polish to decorate her car with wacky designs.

BURGER BIKE

Where else but America could you see a hamburger racing a high heel down the main street? Such weird and wonderful vehicles are all part of the Art Car movement, which boasts hundreds of enthusiasts in cities across the U.S. Harry Sperl relishes driving around Daytona Beach, Florida, on the Hamburger Harley, a 1100cc Harley Davidson trike covered with a huge fiberglass-and-styrofoam hamburger.

RED SHOE-STER

David Crow, a designer from Seattle, Washington, is the proud creator of the amazing Red Stiletto, a dragster-style frame in the shape of a large high heel shoe. Some Art Cars are barely recognizable as cars, like Art the Lobster, designed and built by sculptor A.J. Strasser of Fairfax, Virginia. Building the 35-foot-long fiberglass crustacean took him more than six years.

Ripley Replay
October 7, 1933

Charles Miller lived in a mobile home, 6 feet by 3 feet 9 inches, for nearly three years.

BRIGHT IDEA

Santiago taxi driver Juan Geraldo has covered every inch of his car's interior with black and white spotted fake cowhides, including the steering wheel and roof. He hopes the car will look so conspicuous that nobody will dare rob him.

DOUBLE TAKES

NO PLACE LIKE GNOME

Ron Broomfield is a giant among men—at least he is among the hundreds of colorful little garden gnomes that share his home and garden in Alford, Lincolnshire, England. But not only does Ron collect gnomes, he likes to think he is one! So twice a week, he dresses up as a gnome by putting on a bright red cap, a yellow waistcoat, red trousers with green patches, and white boots. He then adds a pipe and a fishing rod and joins his miniature porcelain friends in the garden among tiny toadstools and whirling windmills. Ron's house, naturally enough called Gnome Cottage, is crammed with his collection of around 1,000 gnomes. He has spent more than $33,000 on his hobby.

TURTLE POWER!

Michele Ivey of Ferndale, Michigan, sees herself as the fifth Ninja Turtle. Her obsession began in 1989 when she watched *Teenage Mutant Ninja Turtles* on the TV. Michele, then aged 11, was instantly hooked and fell madly in love with the turtle with the green mask, Michelangelo, the party animal of the gang. Since then, she has stockpiled every kind of Ninja Turtle merchandise, including comics, toys, and movie scripts. Every Christmas, she asked for turtle toys and she even spent $5,000 on karate lessons so that she could copy her heroes. Now in her late twenties, she still adores the turtles and her house is a shrine to them with posters and models everywhere.

Full Of Beans

Barry Kirk is no ordinary human bean. He is so crazy about baked beans that he has officially changed his name to Captain Beany. He dresses in an orange jumpsuit and cape, with his bald head painted orange, and drives a car decorated with baked bean artwork. In fact, Captain Beany has become a superhero crusader working for charitable causes near his home in Port Talbot, South Wales. And the man who claims to hail from the Planet Beanus doesn't stop there. He drinks baked bean cocktails, regularly takes the plunge in a bath full of baked beans and tomato sauce, and has turned his apartment into a bean museum! And, of course, he eats baked beans every single day. Just to make sure that his home planet doesn't try to reclaim him, he has also taken the precaution of insuring himself for $750 against alien abduction. Bean me up!

137

PAINTING PRODIGY

Akiane Kramarik of Sandpoint, Idaho, has been drawing and painting amazing pictures since she was four. She began working in pastels at age five and a self-portrait that she painted at seven was sold for $10,000.

HIGH FLIER

While most 11-year-old boys are mastering skills like baseball, basketball, or football, Xavier Gouin (left) was already a qualified pilot at that age. And though he may have been Europe's youngest pilot, he was no match for Emma Houlston, who flew a plane across Canada in 1988—at the age of nine! More recently, in October 2005, Parker Henderson of California made his first solo flight, at the age of 14. With such talent, the sky's the limit for these young pilots.

BAY WATCH

At the age of just seven, Braxton Bilbrey swam from Alcatraz to San Francisco in May 2006. Although he's only a little over four feet tall and weighs about 65 pounds, the boy from Arizona swam the 1.4 miles in 47 minutes. He was accompanied by his coach and two other strong adult swimmers in case he had any difficulties. Braxton, who thought his achievement was "pretty cool," had the idea after reading about a nine-year-old who had made the swim.

YOUNG SPIELBERG

You often see child actors at the movies, but Kishan Shrikanth is a child director! The Indian boy was just 10 years old when he directed his first film, *C/O Footpath*, in 2006. Kishan, who also co-wrote the screenplay about India's slum children, says he had no trouble dealing with adult actors like Bollywood star Jackie Shroff. "They listen to me, so I don't find it difficult to run the show on the sets. They treat me like any other director."

Ripley Replay
August 31, 1947

This young boy was so strong he could hold himself horizontal with his feet off the ground!

INDEX

PHOTO CREDITS: Ripley Entertainment Inc. and the editors of this book wish to thank the following photographers, agents, and other individuals for permission to use and reprint the following photographs in this book. Any photographs included in this book that are not acknowledged below are property of the Ripley Archives and MKP Archives. Great effort has been made to obtain permission from the owners of all materials included in this book. Any errors that may have been made are unintentional and will gladly be corrected in future printings if notice is sent to Ripley Entertainment, Inc., 7576 Kingspointe Parkway, Suite 188, Orlando, Florida 32819.

COVER/ TITLE PAGE: Marco Hort—Vladimir Kmet/AFP/Getty Images

TOC: Can Butterfly—Empics; Tallest and Shortest Men—Rex Features

PAGE 4: Ripley Archives

PAGE 5: Ripley Archives

PAGE 6: Tin Pheasants, Enchanted Highway—Gary Greff; Toilet Restaurant, Reuters/Joe Tan; Look-alike—Getty Images; Two-headed Turtle—Getty Images

PAGE 7: Ripley Archives

Chapter 1: 9, 12: Signpost Forest—Quaisse Philippe/Camera Press; **10:** Fremont Troll—Troll photo courtesy of John Cornicello; **10–11:** Cabazon Dinosaurs—Newscom; **11:** Water Tower—Strickland Photography; **13:** Gopher Hall Museum—Torrington Tourism Action Society; Tin Pheasants, Enchanted Highway—Gary Greff; Tin Men, Enchanted Highway—Gary Greff; **14:** Cloud Gate—Howard Ash; **15:** Inflatable Church—Rex Features; **16:** Petrified Wood—James Randklev/Corbis; **17:** White Desert—Reuters/Tara Todras-Whitehill; **18:** *Floralis generica*—Ana Scannapiecp/Lisandro Penecas; Big Head—Wattie Cheung/Camera Press; **19:** Mechanical Elephant—Getty Images; **20:** Giant Cookie—Louie Psihoyos/Corbis; **20–21:** Huge Saucepan—Reuters/Alberto Lowe; **21:** Hershey's Kiss—The French Culinary Institute

Chapter 2: 23, 33: Day of the Dead—Danny Lehman/Corbis; **24:** Geronimo—Bettmann/Corbis; **25:** Skeleton—Michael Williams; **26:** George lll—Topfoto; Hitler's Teeth—Getty Images; **27:** Model Head—Martin Pope/Camera Press; Bog Mummy—Empics; **28:** Cellphone Tombstone—Rex Features; **28–29:** Shark Coffin—Getty Images; **29:** Exploding Ashes—Reuters/Pool New; **30:** Roman Forum—Bryce Newell/Fotolia.com; **31:** Skeleton—Chris Harvey/Fotolia.com

Chapter 3: 35, 44: Tomatina Festival—Reuters/Desmond Boylan; **36:** Look-alike—Getty Images; **37:** Noodles—Newscom; Giant Poori—Reuters/Arko Datta; **38:** Underwater Music—Getty Images; Margate Grotto; **39:** Pumpkin Carving—Getty Images; **40:** Tombstone—Killroy/Fo-

tolia.com; **42–43:** Crazy Moustache—Getty Images; **44:** Cheese Rolling—Getty Images; **45:** Huhu Grub—Juergen Schacke

Chapter 4: 47, 54: Elephant Soccer—Reuters/Chaiwat Subprasom; **48:** Skydiving Dog—Tom Sanders/Barcroft Media; **49:** Tigers and Rabbits—Reuters/China Daily China Daily Information Corp–CDIC; Diving Horse—Empics; **50:** Mandrill Monkey—Reuters/Str Old; **51:** Water-holding Frog—Chris Mattison, Frank Lane Picture Agency/Corbis; **52:** Art in Lion Cage—Reuters/Philippe Wojazer; **53:** Bald Baboon—Rex Features; **55:** Water-skiing Squirrel—Getty Images; Tightrope Cat—Dee Hunter, Hunter Photography 2006; **56:** Barbary Monkey—Getty Images; **56–57:** Peacock—Suzan Oschmann/Fotolia.com; **57:** Emperor Penguin—Fabrice Beauchene/Fotolia.com; **58:** Four-legged Chicken—Duan Renhu/Phototex/Camera Press; **59:** Two-headed Goat—Reuters/STR New; Two-headed Turtle—Getty Images

Chapter 5: 61, 66: Ice Sculpture—Empics; **62–63:** Cats—Reuters/Sergo Edisherashvili; **63:** Panda—Empics; **65:** Window Reflection—Anna Sirotina/Fotolia.com; Bulldog—Steven Pepple/Fotolia.com; **66:** Sand Sculpture—Empics; **67:** Can Butterfly—Empics; **68:** Postboxes—Rex Features; **70–71:** Chocolate Mosque—Reuters/Supri Supri; **72:** Mona Lisa—Reuters/Claro Cortes

Chapter 6: 75, 80: Grasshopper in Mouth—Robin Utrecht/ANP/Camera Press; **76:** Scorpion Woman—Cedric Arnold/Camera Press; **77:** Man Covered in Bees—Reuters/Beawiharta Beawiharta; Snake—Javed Jafferji/Camera Press; **78:** Marco Hort—Vladimir Kmet/AFP/Getty Images; **79:** Man Breaking Concrete—Getty Images; Needles in Head—Rex Features; **80:** Christmas Dinner—Rex Features; **81:** Toilet Restaurant, Reuters/Joe Tan; **82:** Man in Box—Getty Images **83:** Tennis-racket Contortionist—Getty Images; **84:** Funny Fingernails—Reuters/Kamal Kishore; **85:** Metal Mouth—Empics; Back Piercings—Newscom

Chapter 7: 89, 92: Pulling Car—Photoshot; **90:** Frozen Landscape—Marcviln/Fotolia.com; Aeroplane—Hartmut Lerch/Fotolia.com; **91:** Skydiver—Newscom; **92:** Suspended Car—Rex Features; **93:** Car Crash—Rex Features; **96–97:**

Python Playmate—Reuters/Chor Sokunthea; **98:** Tanya Streeter—Empics; **99:** Unusual Golf—Getty Images; Alain Robert—Empics

Chapter 8: 101, 105: Dancing Robot—Getty Images; **102:** White Python—Reuters/Chor Sokunthea; **103:** Gila Monster—NHPA; **104:** Fly—Adrien Roussel/Fotolia.com; **105:** One-cent Coin—ILLYCH/Fotolia.com; **106:** Bacteria Glue—Yves Brun/courtesy Indiana University; **107:** Cow Urine—Reuters/Chor Sokunthea; **108–109:** Squirting Milk—Reuters/Sean Yong; **110:** Tallest and Shortest Men—Rex Features; Little Man—Reuters/STR New; **111:** Hairy Face—Empics; **113:** Face Transplant—Franck Crusiaux/Gamma/Camera Press; Operation Zero—Reuters/Ho New

Chapter 9: 115, 122–123: Mummy Museum—Reuters/Francois Lenoir; **116:** UFOs—Michel Piccaya/Fotolia.com; **117:** UFO Under Plane Wing—Topfoto; UFO Landing Port—Roadside America.com; Black and White UFO picture—Rex Features; **118:** Girl jumping—Topfoto; **119:** Ship—Empics; Seeing Double—Topfoto; **120:** Haunted Shoes—Rex Features; **121:** Abraham Lincoln—Getty Images; **124:** Catacombs—Getty Images; Jewelry—Getty Images; **125:** Pet Cemetery—Getty Images; **126:** Snowman—Guy Verville/Fotolia.com; **126–127:** Beefeaters—Reuters/Lynn Fergusson; **127:** Giant Rabbit—Gelitin

Chapter 10: 129, 137: Captain Beany—Roger Donovan/Media Photos/Camera Press; **130:** Car Tower—Car Tower Autostadt, Rainer Jensen; **131:** Roses—Vaide/Fotolia.com; Pet Bird—Getty Images; **132:** Musical-instrument Car—Hunter Mann; **132–133:** Hamburger Harley—Harrod Blank; **133:** Red Stiletto Car—Harrod Blank; **134–135:** Cow Fabric Interior—Reuters/Ivan Alvarado; **136:** Gnome Man—Rex Features; Teenage Mutant Ninja Turtle—Empics; **138:** Young Pilot—Deville Marc/Camera Press; **139:** Swimmer—Frederic Larson/San Francisco Chronicle/Corbis; Young Director—Getty Images